A Mystery of Nature Series

The Mystery of Wildhorse Island

By Randy Persson

Illustrated by Sheila Somerville

INKWELL BOOKS
Writing-Publishing-Printing

Mysteries of Nature Series
Mystery of Wildhorse Island

ISBN: 978-1-7366445-5-3
Library of Congress Control Number: 2020991857

Published by Inkwell Books, LLC
10632 North Scottsdale Road, Unit 695
Scottsdale, AZ 85254
Tel. 480-315-3781
E-mail info@inkwellbooksllc.com
Website www.inkwellbooksllc.com

Illustrations by Sheila Somerville

INKWELL BOOKS
Writing-Publishing-Printing

Randy grew up enjoying the forests and lakes of Minnesota and the deserts of Arizona. A book lover, Randy was a co-owner of a large used bookstore in Phoenix, Arizona. The bookstore was a "wonderful place to work and we dedicated 25% of the store to children's books. We had a 'free box' outside the store and each night we would put a couple of used children's books in it and always found it empty the next morning. We tried very hard to get books into the hands of everyone, whether they could afford them or not."

Randy, his wife Rose, their children and grandchildren all live in Arizona. Our family hopes that you will enjoy this book and, at a minimum, keep reading!

DEDICATION

To my sons, Taylor and Drew, for their curiosity and inspiration on solving Nature's Mysteries.

Love you!

My name is Taylor and I am ten years old. This is the story of a trip my brother Drew and I took last summer to a place called "Wildhorse Island."

Drew helped me out with this story. He remembers quite well for a little kid. Since he's only five, he was not able to help me too much with the spelling.

The story is real and so is the mystery.

The Mystery of Wildhorse Island

Drew and I were excited about our summer vacation. We were going to visit Grandpa Al and Grandma Rose in Montana.

Before we left, I looked up Montana in the encyclopedia and learned that it is in the northwestern part of the United States. The state of Montana is loaded with beautiful pine forests and cold rivers full of trout and salmon.

What the encyclopedia did not say was that there are mysteries in Montana. But then, I am old enough to know that there are mysteries almost everywhere!

Grandpa and Grandma met us at the Missoula Airport and from there, we drove to Flathead Lake. Drew and I were excited but we managed to behave ourselves in the car, only asking Grandpa to stop two or three times so we could go to the bathroom, get ice cream cones, and things like that.

When we got to the lake, I was amazed at how big it was. We were standing on the shore of an inlet called "Big Arm Bay." My brother was staring across the blue water.

"Is that a mountain?" he asked Grandpa, pointing to a large rock and tree-covered hill across the water.

Grandpa smiled. "That's Wildhorse Island," he said.

Grandpa told us that the local people named it "Wildhorse Island." Then he asked us why they would called it that.

My brother said, "Because it has wild horses on it?"

Wow. Sometimes my brother can be a real pain. "Horses can't swim that far, Drew," I told him. "How could there be wild horses out there?"

My brother shrugged and said, "Then why do they call it 'Wildhorse Island'?"

I thought for a minute and said, "Maybe it's named after an Native American named 'Chief Wildhorse.' There probably used to be Native Americans here, huh Grandpa?"

Grandpa smiled and said there were indeed several tribes in this area, but that wasn't where the island got its name.

Before my brother and I could get into a big argument about how the island got its name, Grandpa

had the boat ready to go. We put on our life jackets and climbed in.

It was a calm and sunny day and the Montana sky was bright blue. My brother and I loved being on the water in Grandpa and Grandma's boat. We were looking at the beautiful scenery when suddenly, a large bird came diving down out of the blue sky! It swooped along the surface of the water and grabbed a huge fish right out of the lake!

"Wow!" Drew exclaimed as the bird flew away, holding the fish in its large claws. "That bird really knows how to catch fish!"

Grandpa said the bird was an osprey and that it was probably taking food back to its young.

"Do they eat it raw?" my brother asked.

I looked at him. "No, genius, they cook it in the microwave first!"

Grandpa laughed. "Yes, Drew, they eat it raw."

"Yuck," my brother said.

As we got close to the island, Grandpa steered the boat along the shoreline. When we approached a small inlet, my brother and I both yelled, "Wow! Look!"

There on the shore, standing by the water, were two white-tailed deer. They snapped to attention when we yelled. Their ears stood up and twitched. They looked right at us, then turned and in two or three quick leaps, disappeared into the woods.

"We'll have to be very quiet if we want to see wildlife here," Grandpa said. "These animals aren't used to seeing many people."

My brother and I both felt bad for yelling.

"I hope they were done drinking water," I said.

We began to go around the northwest corner of the island and we saw what looked like a wooden box high in a tree near the shoreline.

"What's that, Grandma?" I asked. She said that it was a nest for Canadian Geese.

My brother scratched his head. "How can a goose use hammers and nails and saws and stuff?" (Sometimes I don't know how my brother thinks up such things.)

Grandma explained that the box was made by a group of students from a Missoula High School. It seems that geese do not make very strong nests and sometimes the eggs fall out, so the kids at the high school were helping the geese by making these boxes where the geese could build safe nests.

"What a great idea. It's like they have their own tree house," I said.

"And the bears can't get them!" added Drew.

Halfway around the north side of the island we approached a rocky area with large cliffs rising out of the water. Once again, my brother and I saw something and we were about to shout, but we remembered Grandpa's warning.

Excitedly, we pointed to some brown and white animals that were climbing up the rock.

"Those are wild sheep," Grandma whispered.

Drew and I watched the small herd as it moved single file up the rocky ledges. They were amazingly sure-footed. The animals seemed to dance on their nimble legs.

We saw two baby sheep in the little herd. They were closely following their mother. Grandma told us that was how they learned to walk on the steep, rocky cliffs.

After we turned down the east side of Wildhorse, Grandma got a fishing rod, put on a lure, and dropped the line in the water behind the boat. "We use barbless hooks," she explained, "because we catch and release the fish. We don't want to hurt them with the hook."

Next, we said the Fish Chant, which Grandma had taught us.

Bastachuttes, Bastachuttes, Bastachuttes!

Hulla, Hulla, Hulla!

Just like magic, the fishing rod bent over toward the water! Drew jumped up and down with excitement as Grandma helped me reel in the fish. It was a beautiful lake trout.

I wanted to keep it, but we had to let it go. I was sad, but the fish looked relieved to be back in the water.

We passed the old hotel and came to the southeast corner of the island. Grandpa pointed to a tall pine that seemed to tower above the shoreline. At the top, a big limb was sticking straight up like a finger.

"Look carefully," he told us. "What do you see?"

My brother and I squinted at the tree. At first we did not see anything except the bare limbs of the tree. But then . . . one of the limbs moved! A large, brown, shiny bird was perched at the very top of the highest limb.

"That's a bald eagle!" Grandpa whispered. I knew from school that the bald eagle is a symbol for the United States. This one did not have white feathers on its head like the ones I had seen in pictures.

Grandpa explained that the young eagles are all brown. When they are three years old, they grow new white feathers on their heads.

We had gone almost all the way around the island when Grandpa said, "Well, how do you think those deer and sheep got on the island?"

Drew said he was still trying to figure out why it was called Wildhorse Island. I nodded my head in agreement. There were no bridges or anything going to the island, so I told Grandpa that I couldn't figure out how the sheep and deer got here.

"Well," Grandpa said, "there's more than sheep and deer. There are beavers, squirrels, foxes, skunks, chipmunks, and other animals on the island."

My brother and I strained our brains, thinking about how all those animals could possibly get to the island. Drew's eyes lit up. "Maybe UFOs came and picked up the animals in the forest and carried them to the island!" he said.

Before I could even tell him what a goofy idea

that was, Grandpa was holding his finger to his lips. "Ssshhh! Look!"

"Horses!" I responded excitedly, as quietly as I could. My brother blinked his eyes and nodded his head.

"Wow," he whispered. Up by the trees, on a rocky ledge, were three horses.

"How did they get here, Grandpa?" I asked.

"Don't tell, don't tell!" my brother whispered. "I figured it out!"

Grandpa laughed. "Okay, Drew, how did they get here?"

Drew couldn't take his eyes off the horses, he was so fascinated with them. "It gets cold here in the winter, right?" he whispered softly so the horses couldn't hear him and run off.

"Right," Grandpa said.

"And it snows a lot and the lake water can freeze like an ice cube, right?"

"Right," Grandpa said.

I couldn't believe it. My little brother had figured it out before me!

"You figured it out, Drew," Grandpa said. Some winters are very cold and if the water freezes, it forms an ice bridge across the lake. The animals walk over on the ice, perhaps looking for food or shelter . . ."

I finished his thought. "And in the spring, when the ice melts, the animals get stranded on the island!"

"Very good," complimented Grandpa.

My brother sneered at me. "Very good, Taylor, but I figured it out first!"

I had to admit, he was right.

We watched the horses graze on the green grass near the rocky ledge. They looked just like the horses you see at ranches, except they were wild.

Grandpa said they might be part of a herd that has been on the island for a long time, for many generations of horses – maybe fifty years or longer.

"Wow," Drew said. "that's a long time ago! Were there still dinosaurs here in those days?"

I rolled my eyes at Grandpa. My brother might have figured out the mystery of Wildhorse Island, but he didn't know everything!

Grandpa smiled. "Well," he said, "fifty years ago was not that long ago. In fact it was about fifty years ago when I first saw wild horses on the Wildhorse Island. And I can assure you, there were no dinosaurs here then!"

Grandpa, Grandma, my brother and I spent the rest of the afternoon exploring the island. We saw tracks in the soft earth near the water. Grandpa identified them as being made by the raccoons, deer and wild sheep we had seen. When we found a lot of roundish tracks, I asked Grandpa if they were from the wild horses. Grandpa said they were.

My brother said we should look for dinosaur tracks, too, but Grandpa said it was getting late and we should get in the boat and head for home.

"Just because you figured out one mystery," I said to Drew, "doesn't mean you're some kind of genius. There are no dinosaur tracks on Wildhorse Island."

"Probably not," Grandpa said, "but there are still plenty of mysteries to be solved. Next time you come up, we'll see if you two can solve another one."

Drew and I excitedly agreed. "And next time," I

told Drew, "I'll bet I will figure out the mystery before you do!"

The sky was getting darker and the wind was beginning to blow. Grandma Rose said we should go back to the cabin and have some hot cocoa. That was a great idea and Drew and I forgot all about any more mysteries.

Until the next time, that is.

www.ingramcontent.com/pod-product-compliance
Lightning Source LLC
Chambersburg PA
CBHW040856100426
42813CB00015B/2810